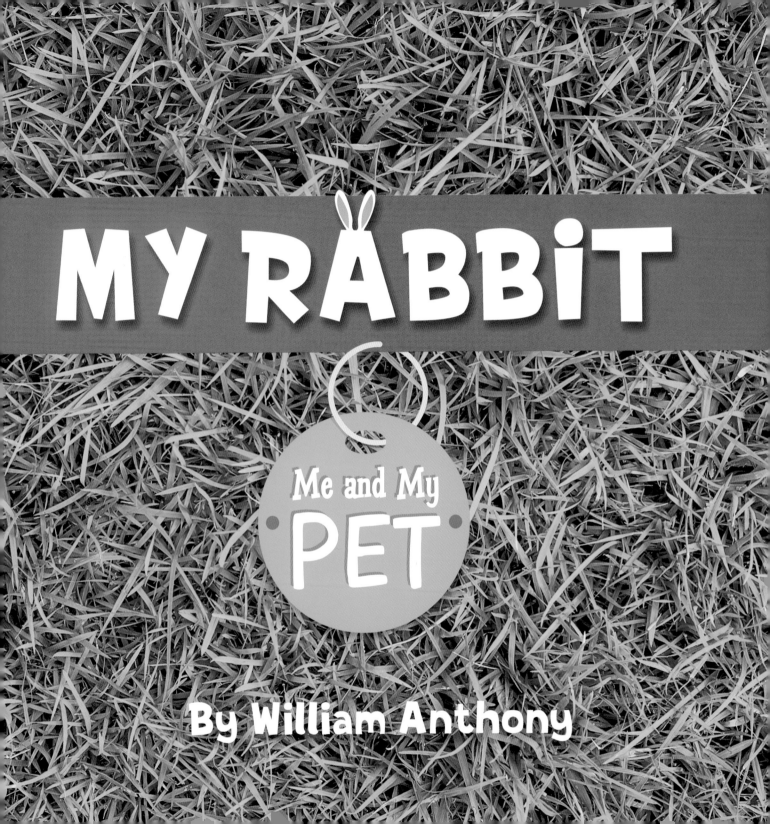

MY RABBIT

Me and My
PET

By William Anthony

BookLife
PUBLISHING

©2019
BookLife Publishing Ltd.
King's Lynn
Norfolk PE30 4LS

ISBN: 978-1-78637-573-5

Written by:
William Anthony

Edited by:
Robin Twiddy

Designed by:
Jasmine Pointer

CONTENTS

Words that look like this can be found in the glossary on page 24.

Chloe and Scotch

Hello! My name's Chloe, and this is my pet rabbit, Scotch. He's seven years old. Rabbits are my favourite animal because they are soft, friendly, and I love the way they hop!

Chloe

Scotch

Whether you're thinking about getting one, or you've had one for a little while, Scotch and I are going to take you through how to look after a rabbit!

Lead the way, Scotch!

Getting a Rabbit

Looking after a rabbit means you are going to have a lot of **responsibility**. You will need to feed them, and give them a nice home with a warm bed.

Scotch's Hutch

Take your time choosing your rabbit; you will be friends for a long time!

My family got Scotch from a pet shop, but you can get rabbits from lots of places. You can get them from someone who **breeds** them, or from a **rescue centre**.

Home

When you first get your rabbit, you need to decide whether you will keep them indoors or outside. Rabbits can live in either place.

If you keep your rabbit outside, they'll need a hutch with lots of hay to keep warm. If you keep your rabbit indoors, make sure you hide wires and make everywhere safe!

Playtime

Rabbits are very curious
(say: cure-ee-us), which
means they like to explore.
It's good to give them lots
of things to play with.
This keeps their minds
busy all day long.

A comfortable rabbit is a happy rabbit!

When you're petting your rabbit, it's important to be soft and gentle with them. You might frighten them if you are **rough** with them or shout a lot!

11

Food

Hay is just grass that has dried out!

Feeding your bunny isn't too hard. Rabbits are called grazing (say: gray-zing) animals, which means they mostly eat grass and hay.

As well as grass and hay, rabbits need a little bit of **variation** (say: vare-ee-ay-shun) in their **diet**. You can buy rabbit food from a pet shop.

Make sure you put some water in their bottle too!

Bedtime

If your rabbit
lives outside in a hutch,
they will need lots of bedding to stay
warm at night. It can get very cold in winter.

Rabbits like to sleep in lots of hay, straw, sawdust or paper. Every rabbit will have their favourite. It's important to try each type of bedding out and see which one they like best!

The Vet

Vets are like doctors, but for animals instead of humans!

Rabbits can get ill, just like humans. Rabbits that are ill can go to the vets. The vet will do everything they can to help your rabbit get better again!

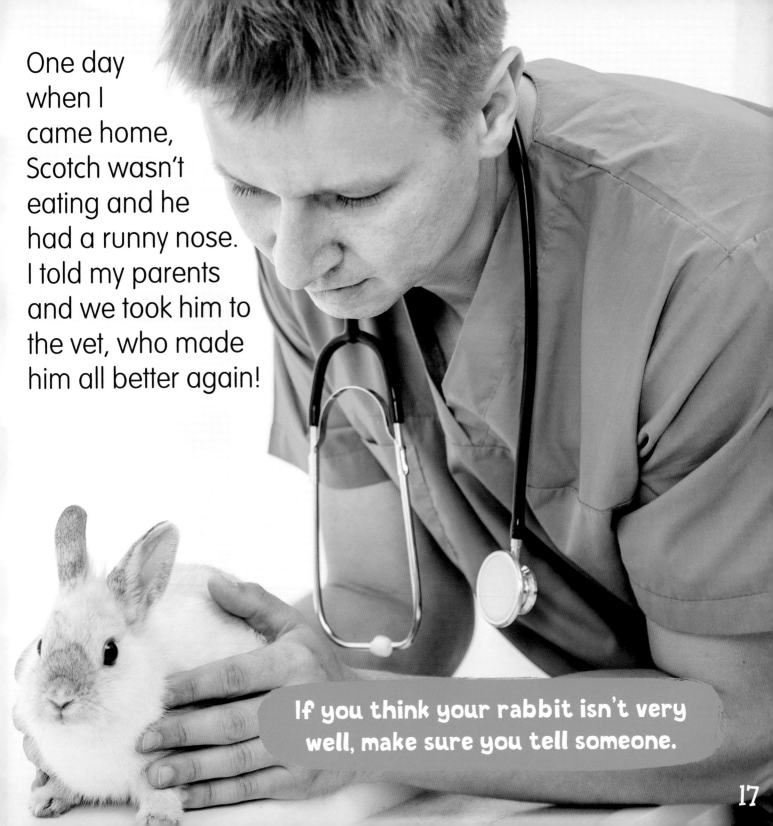

One day when I came home, Scotch wasn't eating and he had a runny nose. I told my parents and we took him to the vet, who made him all better again!

If you think your rabbit isn't very well, make sure you tell someone.

17

Growing Up

Not all rabbits live for the same amount of time. Some live for around 10 years, but others have lived to the age of 18! Keep an eye on your bunny to find out when they are getting old.

Your rabbit will sleep much more and eat much less when it is old.

Make sure older rabbits are as comfortable as possible.

When your bunny is getting old, you need to be gentle with them and give them lots of hugs. Try to get them to <u>exercise</u> as much as possible to keep them healthy.

Super Rabbits

All rabbits are amazing, but some bunnies are super rabbits! Bini the Bunny lives in the US, and he can paint his own works of art!

Bini also holds the world record for the most basketball slam dunks in one minute by a rabbit. He scored seven!

You ♥ and Your Pet

Whether your rabbit is a normal rabbit or a super rabbit, make sure you take care of them just like Scotch and I have taught you!

I'm sure you'll make a great pet owner. Have fun with your new fluff-ball. If you had a super rabbit, what would be the first world record you would try to break?

GLOSSARY

breeds	takes care of animals in order to make more animals
diet	the kinds of food that an animal or person usually eats
exercise	physical activity that is done to become stronger and healthier
rescue centre	a place that helps animals that have had a difficult life find a new loving home
responsibility	having tasks that you are expected to do
rough	causing or likely to cause harm or injury; not gentle
variation	a change to what is normal

INDEX